CAREERS IN
STEM

Computer Programmer

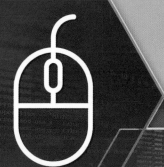

by Elizabeth Noll

BLASTOFF!
READERS
3

BELLWETHER MEDIA • MINNEAPOLIS, MN

Blastoff! Readers are carefully developed by literacy experts to build reading stamina and move students toward fluency by combining standards-based content with developmentally appropriate text.

Level 1 provides the most support through repetition of high-frequency words, light text, predictable sentence patterns, and strong visual support.

Level 2 offers early readers a bit more challenge through varied sentences, increased text load, and text-supportive special features.

Level 3 advances early-fluent readers toward fluency through increased text load, less reliance on photos, advancing concepts, longer sentences, and more complex special features.

★ **Blastoff! Universe**

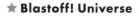

Reading Level

Grade **K**

Grades **1–3**

Grade **4**

This edition first published in 2023 by Bellwether Media, Inc.

No part of this publication may be reproduced in whole or in part without written permission of the publisher. For information regarding permission, write to Bellwether Media, Inc., Attention: Permissions Department, 6012 Blue Circle Drive, Minnetonka, MN 55343.

Library of Congress Cataloging-in-Publication Data

LC record for Computer Programmer available at: https://lccn.loc.gov/2022005449

Text copyright © 2023 by Bellwether Media, Inc. BLASTOFF! READERS and associated logos are trademarks and/or registered trademarks of Bellwether Media, Inc.

Editor: Betsy Rathburn   Designer: Andrea Schneider

Printed in the United States of America, North Mankato, MN.

Table of Contents

Behind the Game

The new video game is almost done. A team of computer programmers works on the final touches.

They test the **software**. It works! The game can be sold!

testing software

What Is a Computer Programmer?

app

Computer programmers make software. They make **apps**. Some create websites. Some make video games!

They work for businesses and schools. They may also work for the government.

Famous Computer Programmer

Name • Linus Torvalds

Born • December 28, 1969

Birthplace • Helsinki, Finland

Schooling • University of Helsinki

Known For • made Linux, a free software that lets anyone work with and change the code

Software is made up of **code**.
Code tells computers what
to do.

code

Programmers write code. They test it, too. They cut out parts that do not work.

At Work

Programmers often work on teams. They work with **engineers** and **designers**.

They talk about projects. They share ideas and fix problems. They also plan future projects.

designers

They run tests on software. They find **bugs** and other problems.

They **update** software to keep it working. They make sure software is **secure**. This lets people safely use it!

Computer Programming in Real Life

working websites

video games

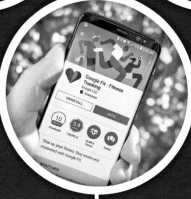

safe apps

Programmers **adapt** software. They make sure it can run on different phones and computers.

Using STEM

Science — test ideas about what computers can do

Technology — use computers to find software problems

Engineering — make new software for computers

Math — use math to solve problems

They make software more **accessible**. This makes sure everyone can use it!

Becoming a Computer Programmer

Programmers are good at solving problems. They look closely at tiny details.

They must know **programming languages**. Each language has its own uses. Some people learn these on their own!

programming
language

```
ength)

SourceIndex
x, EndIndex

                                         uments']

        state'] == 'present':
         put(

      (module.params['login_user'],module.p
    rs = { "content-type": "application/jsc
    = json.dumps({
   "durable": module.params['durable'],
   "auto_delete": module.params['auto_delet
   "internal": module.params['internal'],
   "type": module.params['exchange_type'],
   "arguments": module.params['arguments']
   })

   arams['state'] ==
```

Many programmers go to college. They study math and **computer science**.

Some work as **interns**. They learn from **expert** programmers.

computer science class

Then, programmers find jobs.
Some make new software
and apps. Others make
video games.

How to Become a Computer Programmer

1
study computer science
in college

2
learn a programming
language

3
work with expert
programmers

4
find a job

programming a video game

Some programmers go to **graduate school**. They study more about computers. There are many ways to be a programmer!

Glossary

accessible—able to be used by people of all abilities

adapt—to make something able to be used for a new purpose

apps—programs such as games and internet browsers; apps are also called applications.

bugs—mistakes or problems in computer programs

code—programming instructions

computer science—the study of computers and their uses

designers—people who plan how things look

engineers—people with science training who design and build machines, systems, or structures

expert—having a lot of knowledge or experience in something

graduate school—a school where people can study a specialty area after college

interns—people who work at a job to gain work experience

programming languages—sets of instructions used to make computer programs

secure—safe against threats

software—computer programs that do specific tasks

update—to give something the latest version or technology

To Learn More

AT THE LIBRARY

Borgert-Spaniol, Megan. *Invent A Game! And More Coding & Strategy Challenges*. Minneapolis, Minn.: Abdo Publishing, 2021.

Edelman, Brad. *Computer Programming: Learn It, Try It!* North Mankato, Minn.: Capstone Press, 2018.

Noll, Elizabeth. *Coding in Computers*. Minneapolis, Minn.: Bellwether Media, 2019.

ON THE WEB

FACTSURFER

Factsurfer.com gives you a safe, fun way to find more information.

1. Go to www.factsurfer.com.

2. Enter "computer programmer" into the search box and click 🔍.

3. Select your book cover to see a list of related content.

Index

The images in this book are reproduced through the courtesy of: Prostock-studio, front cover (computer programmer); Oleksiy Mark, front cover (background); Issaurinko, p. 3; Frame Stock Footage, p. 4 (inset); Gorodenkoff, pp. 4-5, 6-7, 10 (designers); dennizn/ Alamy, pp. 6 (app), 14 (safe apps); Chuck Nacke/ Alamy, p. 7 (Linus Torvalds); BEST-BACKGROUNDS, p. 8; FluxFactory, pp. 8-9; NDAB Creativity, pp. 10-11; Pira25, pp. 12-13; AFM Visuals, p. 13 (working websites); JJFarq, p. 13 (video games); antoniodiaz, pp. 14-15; Andriy Popov/ Alamy, pp. 16-17; txoko / Alamy Stock Photo, p. 17 (programming language); dotshock, p. 18 (computer science class); VAKS-Stock Agency, pp. 18-19; Roman Samborskyi, pp. 20-21; Pixel-Shot, pp. 20-21 (programming a video game); Robbi, p. 23 (mouse); Vasyl Onyskiv/ Alamy, p. 23 (keyboard).